Personal Finance Course

Alejandro Rivera

/ Alejandro Rivera /

/ Alejandro Rivera /

Introduction to Personal Finance

Personal finances are a crucial aspect of every individual's life as they focus on the effective management of financial resources at a personal level. This discipline covers a variety of topics, from budgeting to investment planning and debt management. The importance of understanding and applying basic financial principles lies in the ability to make informed decisions that positively impact financial well-being over time.

The foundation of personal finance lies in creating a solid budget that reflects monthly income and expenses. This process allows you to identify areas of overspending, set realistic financial goals, and save for the future. Additionally, knowledge of concepts such as compound interest and investment diversification is essential to maximizing long-term financial performance.

Debt management also plays a crucial role in personal finances, as responsible borrowing can help you achieve important goals, such as purchasing a home or investing in education.

However, it is essential to understand the associated risks and avoid excessive debt accumulation.

Additionally, emergency planning and purchasing appropriate insurance are key aspects of personal finances. These elements provide a financial safety net in cases of unforeseen events, such as illness or loss of employment.

In short, an introduction to personal finance involves understanding and applying fundamental principles to achieve optimal financial health. This knowledge empowers people to make informed financial decisions, build wealth, and confidently face economic challenges throughout life.

Importance

Personal finances play a crucial role in the life of every individual as they provide the tools necessary to effectively manage financial resources on a personal level. Understanding and applying basic financial principles is essential to achieving economic stability and improving quality of life. Proper financial planning allows you to establish achievable goals, such as purchasing a home, educating your children or retiring, providing a solid framework for long-term decision-making.

The ability to create and maintain an efficient budget is essential to avoid unnecessary debt and effectively manage monthly income and expenses. Knowledge of concepts such as compound interest and investment diversification helps maximize financial performance and build wealth over time. In addition, personal finances also address debt management, promoting responsible debt that allows you to achieve important financial goals without compromising financial stability.

Emergency preparedness and purchasing appropriate insurance are key aspects of personal finances, providing a financial safety net in unforeseen times. Ultimately, the importance of personal finance lies in empowering people to make informed decisions, reduce financial stress, and enjoy a more secure and prosperous life.

Mindset

The mindset around personal finances plays a crucial role in how individuals approach their financial matters. Developing a healthy financial mindset involves taking a proactive perspective towards money management, recognizing the importance of financial education and informed decision making. Instead of perceiving finances as a burden, those with a positive financial mindset see financial opportunities and challenges as integral to their growth and well-being.

The personal finance mindset also involves cultivating solid financial habits, such as long-term planning, discipline in spending, and the ability to differentiate between needs and wants. Additionally, the willingness to learn and adapt to changes in the economic environment is essential to prospering financially over time. Those with a positive financial mindset also tend to have an entrepreneurial attitude towards income generation, looking for opportunities to invest and increase their income streams.

Emotional management also plays a critical role in the personal finance mindset. Staying calm during times of economic uncertainty and avoiding impulsive decisions are key aspects of a healthy financial mindset. Additionally, the ability to set realistic financial goals and celebrate achievements, no matter how small, helps maintain a positive attitude toward financial management.

In short, the personal finance mindset encompasses a proactive attitude, sound financial habits, adaptability, and intelligent emotional management. Cultivating a positive financial mindset is essential to building a solid foundation that allows individuals to take control of their finances and work toward a prosperous and sustainable financial future.

Smart Decisions

Making smart decisions in personal finances is an essential component of achieving financial stability and building a strong financial future. First, creating a detailed budget is essential to understanding and managing income and expenses. This process provides a clear view of how resources are distributed and makes it easy to identify areas where unnecessary expenses can be saved or reduced.

Additionally, managing debt strategically is crucial. Making informed decisions about loans, credit cards and other financial instruments prevents excessive debt accumulation and its long-term negative consequences. Additionally, prioritizing debts with higher interest rates can help reduce the overall cost of debt.

Smart investing is another key aspect. Understanding basic investment principles, diversifying portfolios, and considering your time horizon are essential steps to maximizing returns and building wealth over time. Continuing financial education also plays a crucial role in making smart decisions, allowing people to adapt to changes in the market and make informed decisions about investing, saving, and retirement planning.

Emergency planning is an integral part of making smart personal finance decisions. Maintaining an emergency fund provides financial security in unforeseen situations, avoiding the need to resort to costly debt. In addition, purchasing adequate insurance for health, home and other critical aspects helps mitigate financial risks.

In short, making smart decisions in personal finances involves taking a strategic approach to money management, from budget planning to debt management, informed investing and emergency preparedness. These decisions form the foundation for a solid and sustainable financial life.

Administration Scheme

An administration scheme is an organizational structure designed to efficiently manage resources and achieve the objectives of an entity. At its core, it comprises the distribution of authority, responsibility, and coordination of activities within an organization. Hierarchy is an essential component of any management scheme, defining lines of command and establishing the relationship between the different levels of the organization.

Strategic planning is another fundamental aspect of an effective management scheme. It involves establishing long-term goals and objectives, identifying the necessary resources and designing strategies to achieve these objectives. Proper coordination of activities and efficient allocation of resources are crucial to ensure successful execution of the strategy.

Communication is a transversal element in any administration scheme. Facilitates the transmission of information between various hierarchical levels and departments, ensuring a clear understanding of roles and responsibilities. Effective communication also promotes a collaborative work environment and encourages efficient problem solving.

Regarding supervision and control, an effective management scheme establishes mechanisms to evaluate performance and guarantee compliance with objectives. This may include feedback systems, key performance indicators (KPIs), and periodic reviews to adjust strategies as necessary.

Flexibility and adaptability are important characteristics of a modern management scheme, especially in a dynamic business environment. The ability to quickly adjust strategies and operations in response to internal or external changes contributes to the long-term sustainability and success of the organization.

In summary, a management scheme encompasses organizational structure, strategic planning, effective communication, supervision and control, and flexibility to adapt to changes. These elements form an interconnected network that drives the performance and efficiency of the organization in achieving its objectives.

Raise awareness with your Family

Raising family awareness about personal finances is essential to foster a solid financial culture and promote economic stability at the household level. By addressing this topic, you establish a solid foundation for making informed decisions, instilling healthy financial habits from an early age. Collectively understanding the importance of savings, budget planning and debt management helps prevent future financial problems and build sustainable wealth.

Family financial awareness also makes it easier to create and maintain shared financial goals. Establishing common financial goals, such as saving for a child's education, buying a home, or planning for retirement, promotes collaboration and mutual support in achieving those goals. Additionally, open communication about financial issues is encouraged, which contributes to joint resolution of challenges and mitigation of potential money-related tensions in the home.

Family awareness is not only limited to daily money management, but also encompasses understanding more advanced concepts such as investing and asset diversification. Providing financial education to family members empowers them to make informed decisions about how to grow their resources and prepare for their financial future.

Additionally, by promoting awareness about the importance of building an emergency fund and the need to have adequate insurance, the family's ability to deal with unforeseen situations and reduce the financial impact of adverse events is strengthened.

In summary, raising family awareness about personal finances is crucial to establishing a solid financial foundation, promoting collaboration in achieving financial goals, and preparing family members to face financial challenges in an informed and cohesive manner.

/ Alejandro Rivera /

Budget

Budgeting is a fundamental tool for effectively managing personal finances and taking control over money. At its core, a budget is a financial plan that details expected income and expenses over a specific period. The first step in creating an effective budget involves identifying and recording all income, including salaries, additional income, and any other sources of money. This process provides a clear view of the amount of financial resources available to allocate to various areas.

Subsequently, it is essential to carefully list all monthly expenses and categorize them, from fixed expenses such as rent, mortgage and utilities, to variable expenses such as food, entertainment and transportation. Categorization makes it easier to identify areas where you can adjust spending and optimize the use of available resources.

A key component of an effective budget is the inclusion of categories for saving and investing. Allocating a portion of income toward savings goals, such as an emergency fund or vacation planning, promotes healthy financial habits and contributes to long-term wealth building.

Constantly monitoring the budget over time is essential to evaluate its effectiveness and make adjustments as necessary. It may involve using financial tools, specialized applications, or simply keeping a manual record of income and expenses. Regular review allows you to identify spending patterns, make adjustments accordingly, and maintain alignment with long-term financial goals.

In short, effective budgeting involves a systematic process of identifying income, categorizing expenses, allocating resources to specific goals, and ongoing monitoring. This proactive approach not only provides immediate financial control, but also lays the foundation for financial stability and the achievement of financial goals over time.

Follow the Plan

Following your plan is a crucial skill for success in any area of life. In the realm of personal finance, adhering to a pre-established plan involves discipline and commitment to specific financial goals. A fundamental aspect of this process is the ability to maintain consistency between financial objectives and daily actions, ensuring that day-to-day decisions are aligned with the long-term vision.

Consistency in following a financial plan contributes to building healthy financial habits. These habits not only include regular savings and prudent spending management, but also resistance to impulsive temptations that could deviate from the established path. Perseverance in following the plan, even when unexpected financial challenges arise, reinforces resilience and adaptability.

Periodic self-assessment is an essential practice in the task of following what is planned. Regularly reviewing progress toward financial goals allows adjustments to be made as necessary. Changes in personal or financial circumstances may arise, and the ability to adapt in an informed manner ensures that the financial plan remains relevant and achievable.

Patience and perseverance are essential virtues when it comes to following a long-term financial plan. Meaningful results often require time and ongoing effort. Maintaining motivation along this path means constantly remembering set goals and celebrating achievements, even small ones, to maintain inspiration and momentum.

In summary, following what is planned in the financial field implies consistency, discipline and adaptability. Setting clear goals, maintaining healthy financial habits, and making adjustments as necessary are key elements to achieving long-term success in managing personal finances.

Saving

Savings are a fundamental pillar in personal financial management, representing the ability to reserve part of current income to ensure future economic well-being. This financial habit is essential for building a financial safety net and the ability to deal with unforeseen events. The first step to effective savings involves creating a realistic budget that clearly identifies income and expenses, allowing you to determine how much can be allocated to savings.

Setting specific savings goals is a key strategy for maintaining discipline and motivation. Whether it's buying a home, raising children, retiring, or building an emergency fund, having clear goals provides a tangible purpose for the act of saving. Diversifying savings goals also allows you to address different financial aspects simultaneously, balancing short- and long-term planning.

Choosing appropriate savings instruments is another important aspect. Savings accounts, certificates of deposit, and money market accounts are common options for short-term savings, while investing in mutual funds, stocks, and bonds may be appropriate for long-term goals. Understanding your personal risk profile and seeking financial advice are key steps when selecting the most appropriate savings vehicles.

Consistency in the habit of saving, regardless of the amount, is essential. Automating transfers to savings accounts can facilitate this process, ensuring that saving is a constant priority. Additionally, reevaluating and adjusting savings goals as personal and financial circumstances change is crucial to maintaining the relevance and effectiveness of the savings plan.

In short, saving represents a powerful tool to build a solid financial future. From creating a realistic budget to setting specific goals and choosing the right financial instruments, effective savings require a combination of discipline, planning and adaptability over time.

/ Alejandro Rivera /

Prioritize your Expenses

Prioritizing expenses is a fundamental strategy in personal financial management that involves consciously and strategically allocating resources to meet the most important needs and goals. The first step in this process is to identify and classify expenses into essential and non-essential categories. Basic needs such as housing, food, and healthcare should be prioritized as they are critical to daily well-being.

Setting clear financial goals is a key component when prioritizing expenses. Whether it's paying off debt, saving for an emergency, or investing for retirement, having specific goals allows you to direct resources toward areas that contribute significantly to long-term financial progress. This clarity of goals makes it easier to make informed decisions about which expenses deserve higher priority.

Regular analysis of spending habits is essential to adjust priorities as personal and financial circumstances change. Periodic review of the budget allows you to identify areas where cuts or adjustments can be made, freeing up resources for the most important financial priorities. Flexibility in resource allocation is crucial to adapt to fluctuations in income and changes in family needs.

Additionally, taking a proactive approach to debt management is integral to prioritizing expenses. Distinguishing between debts with high interest rates and those associated with investments that generate returns can guide decisions about how to allocate resources to maximize financial efficiency.

In short, prioritizing expenses involves a thoughtful and ongoing evaluation of financial needs and goals. From attention to basic needs to focusing on long-term goals, prioritizing expenses is essential to using resources effectively and achieving sustainable financial stability.

/ Alejandro Rivera /

Eliminate Some Expenses

Eliminating unnecessary expenses is a crucial strategy in personal financial management, aimed at optimizing the use of resources and improving financial health. First, it is essential to conduct a detailed analysis of spending habits to identify areas where cuts can be made without compromising essential well-being. This involves reviewing bank statements, monthly bills and receipts to have a complete understanding of where the money is going.

Once superfluous expenses are identified, steps can be taken to reduce or eliminate these items from the budget. This may include renegotiating service contracts, canceling unused subscriptions, and finding cheaper alternatives for everyday products and services. Using expense tracking apps and tools can be helpful in visualizing patterns and making informed decisions about which areas have the greatest potential for savings.

Eliminating unnecessary spending isn't just about saving money in the short term, it's about freeing up resources for more meaningful long-term financial goals. These resources can be directed toward paying off debt, creating an emergency fund, or investing for financial growth. By focusing on financial priorities, you can achieve more efficient use of income and build a solid foundation for long-term financial success.

It is essential to adopt a mindset of constantly reviewing expenses to ensure the sustainability of these financial habits. As personal and financial circumstances evolve, the ability to adapt and adjust the budget to eliminate unnecessary new expenses is crucial to maintaining financial stability over time.

In short, eliminating unnecessary expenses involves a thorough evaluation of spending habits, followed by concrete actions to reduce or eliminate superfluous items. This strategic approach not only frees up immediate resources, but also contributes to more efficient financial management and the achievement of meaningful financial goals.

/ Alejandro Rivera /

Coordination

Coordinating budget with personal goals is a strategic approach that seeks to align daily financial decisions with an individual's long-term goals. This process begins with the clear and detailed identification of personal goals, which can include everything from buying a home and raising children to retirement and creating an emergency fund. Setting specific, measurable goals provides a solid framework for financial planning.

Once goals have been established, it is crucial to create a budget that reflects these priorities. This involves allocating financial resources consciously, ensuring that every dollar spent contributes in some way to achieving a personal goal. Clear categorization of expenses and allocation of specific funds to each goal help ensure consistency between daily actions and long-term goals.

Periodic review of the budget and personal goals is essential to maintain alignment over time. As personal or financial circumstances change, it may be necessary to adjust funding allocations or even modify goals to accommodate new priorities. Flexibility in budget management allows for agile response to life changes and ensures that financial planning is relevant and effective.

Effective coordination between budget and personal goals also involves constant evaluation of the cost-benefit ratio of expenses. Prioritizing financial activities and decisions that directly drive toward personal goals ensures that resources are used efficiently and effectively. This strategic coordination not only contributes to the achievement of financial goals, but also promotes a sense of purpose and control over one's financial life.

In short, coordinating your budget with your personal goals involves a conscious, strategic approach that aligns daily financial decisions with long-term goals. This continuous process of evaluation and adjustment ensures the consistency and effectiveness of personal financial planning.

Use the Banks

Using banks wisely is essential to optimize personal financial management and make the most of the financial services available. First of all, choosing the right banking institution is crucial. Comparing fees, interest rates, and services offered by different banks allows you to make informed decisions that align with individual financial needs and goals. Furthermore, considering aspects such as the accessibility of ATMs and the availability of online services makes it easier to carry out everyday transactions conveniently.

Opening and maintaining proper bank accounts are essential steps in using banking services effectively. Maintaining checking and savings accounts allows you to clearly separate funds for daily expenses from those reserved for long-term savings. Choosing accounts that offer competitive returns and additional benefits, such as cash back or favorable interest rates, contributes to financial growth.

Prudent credit card management is another important facet of using banks wisely. Using credit cards responsibly, paying balances on time and avoiding accumulated debt, helps build a solid credit history. Additionally, taking advantage of the rewards and benefits associated with credit cards can provide additional financial advantages, as long as they are used responsibly.

Financial planning also involves wise use of services such as loans and investments offered by banks. Comparing interest rates, understanding loan terms, and carefully considering investment options are crucial steps. Diversifying investments and conscious debt management contribute to long-term financial health.

Financial security and fraud protection are important concerns when using banking services. Regularly monitoring transactions, using additional security measures such as two-factor authentication, and maintaining sensitive information securely are essential practices to ensure the integrity of bank accounts.

In short, using banks wisely involves a combination of informed choices, prudent account and card management, and thoughtful financial planning. This strategic approach not only optimizes the benefits of banking services, but also contributes to financial stability and the achievement of long-term goals.

/ Alejandro Rivera /

Inflation

Inflation is an economic phenomenon characterized by the widespread and sustained increase in the prices of goods and services in an economy over a period of time. This gradual increase can have various causes, one of the most common being the increase in the money supply without a proportional increase in the production of goods and services. Inflation is measured through consumer price indices (CPI), which reflect the percentage variation in the prices of a representative basket of goods and services.

The effects of inflation can be diverse and affect both consumers and businesses. On the negative side, inflation reduces the purchasing power of money, since more money is required over time to purchase the same amount of goods and services. This can erode the value of savings and negatively impact people on fixed incomes. Furthermore, inflationary uncertainty can lead to suboptimal economic decisions and distort the efficient allocation of resources.

On the other hand, certain moderate levels of inflation can be considered normal in a growing economy. Inflation can provide incentives for spending and investment, as people and businesses can anticipate price increases in the future. However, when inflation is excessive and uncontrolled, it can generate economic and social instability, negatively affecting financial planning and confidence in the currency.

Central banks often use monetary policies to control inflation and keep it within certain targets. Adjusting interest rates and regulating the money supply are common tools used to influence inflation. The balance between maintaining price stability and promoting economic growth is a constant challenge for monetary authorities.

In summary, inflation is a complex economic phenomenon that has significant impacts on individuals, businesses, and the economy as a whole. Its understanding and management are essential to maintain economic stability and preserve the value of money over time.

Investments

Investing part of your money is a key strategy to grow your assets over time and achieve long-term financial goals. Investing involves allocating resources to assets that have the potential to generate returns, such as stocks, bonds, real estate or investment funds. Diversification, or spreading investment across different asset classes, is essential to mitigate risks and optimize portfolio performance.

Before investing, it is essential to conduct a thorough assessment of your risk tolerance, financial goals, and time horizon. Understanding your financial goals and establishing a coherent investment plan will help you select the strategies and assets that best suit your needs. Patience and discipline are crucial virtues in the world of investing, as markets can experience short-term fluctuations, but have historically shown long-term bullish trends.

Financial education is a key component when investing. Becoming familiar with market basics, asset types, and diversification principles will allow you to make more informed decisions. Additionally, seeking professional advice, either from financial advisors or through independent research, can provide valuable information to make more informed investment decisions.

Continuous monitoring of your portfolio is essential. Conducting regular reviews and adjusting your asset allocation as necessary allows you to adapt to changes in the market and in your own financial circumstances. Reinvesting dividends and constantly contributing to your investments are also effective strategies to enhance growth over time.

Investing can also play an important role in retirement planning. Retirement funds, such as individual retirement accounts (IRAs) or 401(k) plans, offer tax advantages and are effective tools for building wealth over the long term.

In short, investing part of your money is a fundamental strategy to build wealth and achieve your financial goals. It requires careful planning, continued education, and patience over time. By doing so, you can harness the growth potential of the financial markets and work towards a stronger financial future.

Income Sources

Diversifying income sources is a critical financial strategy that can provide economic stability and growth opportunities. A common source of income is wage employment, where a salary is received in exchange for labor services. Additionally, self-employed workers and entrepreneurs can generate income through the sale of products or services. This type of income can vary depending on market demand and the effectiveness of business management.

Passive income, such as that earned through investments, is another important source. Stock dividends, bond interest, and property rental income are examples of how capital can generate returns without active investor involvement. This passive income can contribute to long-term wealth accumulation and offer a form of financial security.

Entrepreneurship and asset creation are also potential sources of income. This may include selling digital products, creating online content, intellectual property, or investing in real estate. The ability to generate income from personal creativity and talent provides significant flexibility and can be an additional source of income.

Income from royalties and copyrights is another way to make a profit, especially for those in creative industries. Artists, musicians, writers, and content creators can receive royalties for continued use of their work, providing recurring income over time.

Participation in affiliate programs and affiliate marketing is a common source of income in the digital age. Individuals may earn commissions by promoting third-party products or services through their online platforms. This can be particularly beneficial for those with a strong social media or blog presence.

Education and consulting are also significant sources of income. Those with expertise in specific areas can offer their services as consultants or educators, either independently or through educational institutions.

Knowledge and experience can become valuable assets that generate additional income.

In short, diversifying income sources involves exploring a variety of opportunities, from traditional jobs to passive income, entrepreneurship, and creative assets. This strategy not only provides greater financial stability, but also opens doors to new possibilities and opportunities for economic growth over time.

/ Alejandro Rivera /

Emergency Funds

The emergency fund is an essential component of healthy financial management and a key tool to face unforeseen events and economic crises. This fund consists of a reserve of liquid money specifically intended to cover unexpected expenses, such as emergency repairs, unexpected medical costs, or loss of employment. The main objective is to provide financial security and avoid resorting to debt in times of crisis, which can have long-term financial consequences.

The recommended amount for an emergency fund is generally based on monthly expenses, and many experts suggest saving three to six months of expenses to provide an adequate safety net. This amount may vary depending on job stability, income level, and other individual considerations. Setting a specific and realistic goal for your emergency fund is essential to guide the savings process.

Liquidity is a fundamental attribute of an emergency fund. Savings should be kept in easily accessible accounts, such as savings accounts or money market accounts, to ensure funds are immediately available when the need arises. Although the profitability of these accounts may be limited, the priority is immediate accessibility.

Discipline in contributing regularly to the emergency fund is key to its effectiveness. Automating fund transfers from your main account to your emergency account ensures that saving is a constant priority. Consistency in contributions, even if modest at first, gradually builds up a solid financial cushion.

The emergency fund is not only used for unforeseen situations, but also provides peace of mind and financial confidence. Knowing that there is a reserve available to meet financial challenges reduces the stress related to economic uncertainty. Additionally, having an emergency fund can allow you to make more informed and strategic financial decisions instead of reacting impulsively to crisis situations.

In short, an emergency fund is an essential tool for personal financial health. It provides protection against unforeseen events, prevents the accumulation of unnecessary debt and contributes to long-term economic stability. Cultivating savings discipline and maintaining liquidity are key elements to maximizing the effectiveness of an emergency fund.

Educate Yourself
Constantly

Constant education on relevant topics is an essential component for personal and professional development, and this is especially true in the financial field. Staying informed and up-to-date on financial concepts, investment strategies, changes in tax legislation, and economic trends is essential to making informed and effective financial decisions over time. Ongoing financial education empowers people to better understand their financial situation, plan realistic goals, and adjust strategies based on changing economic circumstances.

Financial education is not only about understanding products and concepts, but also about developing practical skills for daily money management. Learning how to create and follow a budget, understanding the impact of debt, and knowing strategies to save and invest effectively are valuable skills that contribute to sound financial management. The constant acquisition of financial knowledge promotes autonomy and the ability to make informed decisions that align with personal and family objectives.

In a constantly evolving financial environment, continuing education is essential to adapt to new opportunities and challenges. The incorporation of financial technologies, changes in economic policies and fluctuations in markets require an up-to-date understanding to maximize the potential of investments and minimize risks. Continuous training allows people to take advantage of emerging opportunities and anticipate potential obstacles.

Additionally, ongoing financial education is an effective means to prevent common financial mistakes and avoid bad practices. Understanding the risks associated with certain financial products, knowing the tax implications of financial decisions, and learning to critically evaluate financial information are essential to avoiding pitfalls and making better financial decisions.

Financial education also fosters a growth mindset and adaptability in the face of economic challenges. By being informed about various strategies and approaches, people can adjust their financial plans based on changing conditions and learn from past experiences. The ability to constantly learn and adapt is a valuable asset in long-term financial management.

In summary, constant education on financial issues is essential for individual economic empowerment. It facilitates informed decision making, develops practical money management skills, and provides the tools necessary to meet challenges and take advantage of opportunities in a dynamic financial environment.

New Strategies

The constant willingness to try new learning and personal improvement strategies is essential for continued growth and individual development. Admiration for innovation and the search for new approaches reflects a growth mindset, which involves being open to new ideas and willing to leave the comfort zone. Experimenting with different strategies in areas such as education, professional skills or problem solving provides opportunities to discover more effective and efficient methods.

Exploring new strategies encourages creativity and adaptability. When faced with challenges or goals, the ability to experiment with varied approaches allows you to discover innovative solutions and find methods that best fit specific circumstances. This open attitude towards experimentation also helps overcome the fear of failure, as it is recognized that each attempt offers valuable lessons and opportunities for improvement.

The constant admiration for innovation and experimentation goes hand in hand with the development of problem-solving and critical thinking skills. When faced with new strategies, analytical thinking is stimulated and the ability to evaluate situations from different perspectives is strengthened. This active learning process contributes to a more informed and reflective approach to addressing challenges.

The diversification of strategies is also relevant in the professional field. The willingness to try new methodologies and approaches at work can generate efficiency, promote innovation and improve productivity. Furthermore, the ability to adapt to changes in the work environment is essential in a dynamic and constantly evolving business world.

Constant experimentation with new strategies not only enriches individual knowledge and skills, but also contributes to emotional resilience. The willingness to face the unknown and accept challenges nurtures the ability to adapt to changing situations and overcome obstacles with confidence and determination.

In short, always trying new strategies reflects a proactive mindset toward learning and personal growth. This attitude not only drives continuous improvement, but also strengthens adaptability, creativity and resilience on the path to personal and professional success.

Balance

Balancing quality of life and associated expenses is a crucial aspect of personal financial management. Quality of life involves overall satisfaction and well-being, and achieving a healthy balance involves making financial decisions that support the enjoyment of life without compromising financial stability. A thoughtful approach to this balance involves considering how spending directly affects personal satisfaction and long-term happiness.

In the search for quality of life, it is essential to differentiate between needs and desires. Identifying and prioritizing expenses that contribute significantly to overall well-being is essential to avoid unnecessary debt and the accumulation of superfluous expenses. Creating a realistic budget that reflects personal priorities helps you consciously allocate resources and avoid impulsive spending that can compromise financial stability.

Long-term planning is key in managing the balance between quality of life and expenses.

Considering long-term financial goals, such as purchasing a home, raising children, or retiring, allows you to make financial decisions that align with these aspirations. Investing in experiences and activities that contribute to quality of life, rather than just the accumulation of material goods, can also be an effective strategy.

Debt management is a crucial component in this balance. Avoiding excessive debt accumulation allows you to maintain greater financial flexibility and reduces the stress associated with financial obligations. Constantly reflecting on spending decisions and adjusting to changing circumstances helps maintain a sustainable balance between quality of life and financial health.

Investing in physical and mental health also plays a key role in this balance. Spending on activities that promote health and well-being, such as regular exercise, preventive health care, and recreational activities, can have significant positive impacts on long-term quality of life.

In short, finding the right balance between quality of life and spending involves consciously evaluating personal priorities and making financial decisions that support both immediate satisfaction and long-term well-being. Thoughtful planning, differentiating between needs and wants, and prudent debt management are key components to achieving this balance effectively.

Eliminate Debts

Eliminating debt is a crucial task in personal financial management, as debt can be a significant burden that negatively affects economic stability and limits opportunities for growth. The first step to effectively tackling debt is to conduct a thorough analysis of all financial obligations, including outstanding credit card balances, student loans, mortgages, and any other form of debt.

An effective strategy for eliminating debt is to prioritize balances with higher interest rates. Focusing on paying off high-interest debt first can reduce accumulated financial costs and speed up the debt elimination process. This may involve consolidating debt or looking into refinancing options to get more favorable interest rates.

Creating a structured payment plan is essential to staying on track toward eliminating debt. Establishing a detailed budget that includes specific allocations for debt repayment ensures that adequate resources are allocated to this goal. Consistency in payments and constant contribution to reducing outstanding balances are essential to achieve sustainable results over time.

Negotiating with creditors and exploring flexible payment options can be effective strategies, especially in situations of financial difficulty. Many financial institutions are willing to work with debtors to establish payment plans that fit their circumstances, which may include reducing interest rates or creating structured repayment programs.

Changing spending habits and adopting a more frugal approach can free up additional resources to accelerate debt elimination. This involves identifying areas where cuts can be made, contracts renegotiated, and unnecessary expenses avoided. Financial discipline and the willingness to make temporary sacrifices are key in this process.

Financial education also plays an important role in eliminating debt. Understanding fundamental personal finance concepts, such as credit management, the difference between good and bad debt, and the importance of long-term planning, allows you to make informed decisions and avoid falling back into unsustainable debt patterns.

In short, eliminating debt requires a multifaceted approach that involves planning, budgeting, negotiating, and changing spending habits. It is a gradual process that, with commitment and consistency, provides financial relief and lays the foundation for a healthier financial future.

Donations

Donations play a fundamental role in society, representing altruistic acts intended to support individuals, communities or charitable causes. These financial or other contributions, such as time, goods or skills, have the potential to generate significant positive impact in various areas, from social care to medical research and environmental preservation. The motivation to donate can arise from a variety of reasons, such as empathy, personal connection to a cause, or a desire to contribute to the common good.

Donations can be made through charities, NGOs, religious institutions or directly to people in need. Many organizations offer transparency into the use of donated funds, giving donors confidence that their contribution is being efficiently allocated to the cause they support. The diversity of charities and causes allows donors to find areas that resonate with their specific values and concerns.

On the tax front, donations to charities are typically tax deductible, providing an additional incentive for philanthropy. This benefit can be an important consideration for those looking to maximize the impact of their contributions and optimize their financial situation.

In addition to the financial aspect, donations of time and skills are valuable ways to contribute to the well-being of society. Volunteering with local charities, offering professional skills for free or taking part in community projects are effective ways to make a tangible difference and generate a sense of purpose and connection to the community.

Corporate philanthropy is another significant form of donation, where companies allocate financial resources, products or services to social causes. This practice not only contributes to social well-being, but can also improve the company's reputation and strengthen its connection with socially conscious consumers.

In short, donations represent a powerful act of generosity and solidarity that can have a lasting impact on society. Whether through financial contributions, donation of time or skills, philanthropy plays an essential role in addressing social challenges and contributing to collective well-being. The diversity of causes and ways to give allows individuals and organizations to personalize their philanthropic approach and make a difference in areas they consider most meaningful.

Assets

Assets are fundamental elements in the financial and business field, representing resources that have economic value and contribute to the wealth of individuals, companies or other entities. These can be classified into various categories, such as financial assets, which include cash, investments and marketable securities; tangible assets, such as property, real estate and equipment; and intangible assets, which cover patents, trademarks and intellectual property in general.

In the context of personal finance, assets are essential for building wealth and ensuring long-term economic stability. Asset diversification, or spreading investments across different asset classes, is a common strategy to mitigate risks and optimize returns. Investment portfolios typically include a combination of stocks, bonds, real estate, and other financial instruments.

In the business field, assets are essential for the operation and growth of a company. Efficient asset management involves optimizing their use to generate income and maximize shareholder value. Companies can also use depreciation strategies to account for the decline in value of certain tangible assets over time.

Liquid assets, such as cash and cash equivalents, are especially valuable in emergency situations or to take advantage of investment opportunities. Liquidity provides financial flexibility and the ability to respond quickly to changes in the economic environment.

In accounting terms, assets are found on the left side of a balance sheet and represent what an entity owns. They are balanced by liabilities and equity, reflecting the fundamental accounting equation: assets = liabilities + equity. This equation highlights the relationship between what an entity owns, owes, and its net worth.

In summary, assets are essential components in financial management, representing the resources that contribute to economic value and stability. Diversification, efficient management and understanding of different asset classes are key to maximizing returns and mitigating risks.

/ Alejandro Rivera /

Passives

In the financial and accounting field, liabilities are obligations or debts that an entity has with third parties and that must be settled in the future. They can be classified into current liabilities, which are short-term debts that must be paid within one year, and non-current or long-term liabilities, which represent obligations maturing beyond that period. These obligations may include loans, bonuses, accounts payable, outstanding wages, and other financial commitments.

Liabilities are an integral part of an entity's financial structure and are recorded on the right side of a balance sheet, balancing the fundamental accounting equation alongside assets and equity. The relationship between assets, liabilities and net worth is expressed in the basic accounting formula: assets = liabilities + net worth. This equation reflects the accounting equality between the resources owned, the outstanding obligations and the owners' investment.

Effective liability management involves assessing an entity's ability to meet its obligations and strategically planning debt management. The debt-to-equity ratio is a key financial indicator that measures the relationship between debt and equity, providing information about an entity's financial leverage.

The concept of liabilities can also be applied in a broader sense on a personal level, representing individual financial commitments. Prudent personal liability management involves avoiding excessive debt, understanding the associated interest rates, and planning for timely payment of debts.

In business, issuing bonds and taking loans are common methods to finance operations and projects. These liabilities are carefully managed to ensure that the financial burden is sustainable and does not compromise the long-term financial health of the company.

In short, liabilities represent the financial obligations and debts of an entity, whether at the corporate or individual level. Effective liability management involves carefully assessing outstanding obligations, planning for their fulfillment, and ensuring a healthy balance between assets and liabilities in the overall financial structure.

/ Alejandro Rivera /

www.ingramcontent.com/pod-product-compliance
Lightning Source LLC
Chambersburg PA
CBHW031320250726

48656CB00005B/1887